EARTH'S
NATURAL
BIOMES

TUNDRA
BIOMES

Louise and Richard Spilsbury

WAYLAND

www.waylandbooks.co.uk

First published in Great Britain in 2017 by Wayland

Editor: Hayley Fairhead
Design: Smart Design Studio
Map (page 7) by Stefan Chabluk

ISBN: 978 1 5263 0137 6
10 9 8 7 6 5 4 3 2 1

MIX
Paper from
responsible sources
FSC® C104740

Wayland, an imprint of
Hachette Children's Group
Part of Hodder and Stoughton
Carmelite House
50 Victoria Embankment
London EC4Y 0DZ

An Hachette UK Company
www.hachette.co.uk
www.hachettechildrens.co.uk

Printed and bound in China

**All photographs except where mentioned supplied by
Nature Picture Library www.naturepl.com**

p4 and title page(main) Andy Trowbridge; p5(main), cover(main) and title page(tr) Klein & Hubert; p5(inset) Phil Savoie; p6 Phillippe Clement; p7 Neil Lucas; p8, front cover(b) and title page(b) Alex Hyde; p9 and p32(t) Paul Harcourt Davies; p10 and p30(t) Erlend Haarberg; p11(main) Asgeir Helgestad; p12 and imprint page(b) Doug Wechsler; p13 and p32(b) Sergey Gorshkov; p14 and p30(b) Erland Haarberg; p15 Ingo Arndt; p16 Sergey Gorshkov; p17 Jenny E. Ross; p18 Eric Baccega; p19 Markus Varesvuo; p20(main), front cover(tl) and contents(t) Wild Wonders of Europe / Lesniewski; p20(inset) Robert Thompson; p21 David Welling; p22 and contents(b) Eric Baccega; p23 and p31(t) Eric Baccega; p24, front cover(main) and p31(b) Steven Kazlowski; p25, p26, p27 and p28 Bryan and Cherry Alexander; p29, back cover(tl) and imprint page(t) Ingo Arndt.

Photographs supplied by Shutterstock: back cover(tr) and p11(inset) Bildagentur Zoonar GmbH; p27(inset) Karl Umbriaco.

CONTENTS

WHAT IS TUNDRA?

Tundra is a cold, dry and barren biome. The word tundra comes from a word meaning 'treeless plain' in the Finnish language, and the most obvious thing about tundra is that there are no trees.

Treeless plains

Trees cannot survive in tundra because they need far too much water. There is not enough water available in tundra soil for these large plants to grow and survive through the year. But there are lots of plants that do thrive in the chilly, harsh tundra conditions. These include wiry shrubs, such as heathers and bilberries, and tough grasses and sedges, especially in wetter areas. There are scattered patches of spongy mosses on the ground and colourful lichens surviving on the rocks themselves.

Tundra landscapes are treeless plains with the odd barren mountain and dark pool.

Fact Focus: Biome or Habitat?

Biomes are regions of the world that have a similar climate, plants and animals, such as deserts, forests, rivers, oceans, tundra and grassland. A habitat is the specific place in a biome where a plant or animal lives.

Tundra survivors

Many animals manage to survive in the challenging tundra biome. The low plants are teeming with animal life, from spiders and midges to moths and bumblebees. Some of these help to pollinate the plants' flowers so they can make seeds and berries. Hares, lemmings, geese, mountain goats and caribou feast on the tundra plants.

Hunters in the tundra

Tundra is a hunting ground for lots of predators. In the air, eagles and owls fly silently on the lookout for a tasty bird or mammal to catch and eat. On the ground, tundra predators can be as small as shrews or foxes, and as large as wolves and bears.

Amazing Adaptation

Adaptations are body parts or ways of behaving that living things develop over time to help them survive in a biome. Arctic bumblebees shake their wings very, very fast to stay warm as they fly around in the cold air feeding on tundra flowers.

In winter, Arctic foxes have white fur to blend in with snow and ice when hunting birds and other prey. In summer, the fur turns brown for camouflage against the rocks and plants.

WHERE IS TUNDRA FOUND?

The tundra biome covers over one tenth of our planet's area. Most tundra is in Arctic regions, but some is at the tops of mountains worldwide.

Arctic lands

The Arctic is a circular region of Earth centred on the North Pole, which includes the Arctic Ocean. Arctic tundra is the land surrounding this ocean and covers the northernmost parts of North America, Greenland, Europe and Russia. The Arctic is so cold because it is one of the furthest areas on Earth from the Sun. There is only 25 centimetres of actual rainfall each year, which falls during the milder summers.

The rest of the year it snows and the snow freezes on the land. Most water in the soil is frozen for much of the year. Tree roots cannot suck up enough water to survive or grow deep enough to support the tall body of a tree.

At this treeline in Alaska, there is no straight line of conifers marking the end of the taiga and the start of the tundra. Instead, trees are dotted amongst the pink bilberry and heather plants.

Fact Focus: Treelines

Bordering the tundra there is often a treeline. This marks the slightly warmer and wetter conditions beyond which trees can survive. South of the Arctic tundra much of the forest is coniferous forest. This northern forest biome is called the taiga.

Arctic seasons

If you visited Arctic tundra you would need to wrap up warm all year round. Winter temperatures can drop to a freezing -32°C but even in summer it is very chilly. Winters are dark, cold and windy, and last for over half the year. Summers are short but also very light. The northern part of Earth tilts towards the Sun in summer so the Arctic is sunlit for 24 hours a day. No wonder it is called the Land of the Midnight Sun!

Mountain tundra

A smaller part of the global tundra is found below the tops of high mountains. Temperatures fall the higher up a mountain you go. Up high, it is too windy and cold for many plants to survive. Alpine tundra can be found up mountains in cold regions, such as the Himalayas or Alps, but also at the tops of the tallest mountains in hot regions, such as Africa. Alpine tundra starts higher up mountains in warmer parts of the world.

On Mount Kenya, Alpine tundra plants, such as giant groundsel, survive cold nights by closing up their leaves to trap moisture and stop freezing or drying out.

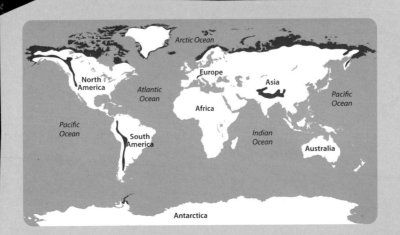

The purple areas on this map show where the tundra biome is found around the world.

ALPINE TUNDRA

Can you imagine living at the top of a cold, windy mountain?
Plants need very special adaptations or features to help them
survive there.

Surviving in the soil

There is little soil on mountain
tops and steep, open slopes
because it is blasted away by
strong winds. Most plants live
on gentle slopes where some soil
has built up. Others survive in
the thin pockets of soil trapped
amongst the exposed rocks of
mountain tops. Plants here rely
on snow cover for insulation
against the cold and to provide
water when the snow melts.

Holding tight

Many Alpine tundra plants
survive the harsh winds by
huddling together and making
themselves smaller. Mosses
grow in compact clumps rather
like cushions close to the
ground, out of the wind. This
tight huddle traps moisture and
warmth to help the individual
plants protect each other and
grow successfully.

Moss campion plants
are cushion-shaped with
overlapping leaves to trap
warmth. Their flowers are raised
above the plant so insects can
pollinate them easily.

Hairy plants

In the cold, the hairs on our arms stand up to trap warm air for insulation. Some Alpine tundra plants use the same trick to survive. Edelweiss plants have a thick, woolly layer of fine strands rather like hairs all over their leaves. The hairy leaves trap heat and protect the plant from the strong sunlight up mountains where they are closer to the Sun.

Amazing Adaptation

Alpine flowering plants develop buds at the end of a short Alpine summer that survive beneath the snow. Next spring, the dark surface of the flower buds absorbs the heat of any sunlight that reaches them through a thin layer of snow. This speeds up the melting of the snow.

The dark colour of Alpine snowbell buds helps the flowers emerge from the snow early so they have time to attract insects and make seeds before winter returns.

Fact File: Northeast Greenland Biosphere Reserve

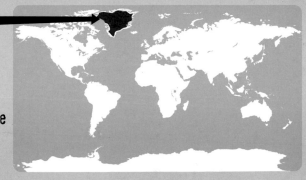

Location: Greenland
Size: 1,000,000 square kilometres
Overview: The largest national park in the world, where tundra animals, such as muskox, polar bears, walrus, snowy owls and ptarmigans far outnumber people.

ARCTIC TUNDRA

Arctic tundra has one enormous difference from Alpine tundra that is hidden beneath the surface — frozen soil or permafrost.

A view of Arctic tundra from the air in summer shows how the land, with its grey rocks and brown grasses, has many pools and patterns made by soil that has been frozen and thawed many times.

Permafrost

Dig down 15 cm or so into Arctic tundra soil and your spade will start to hit hard permafrost, which is hundreds of metres deep over most of the Arctic. The permafrost stays frozen all year round, but during the Arctic summers, a depth of up to three metres thaws out. The meltwater then makes tundra soil extremely boggy.

Summer growth

Arctic tundra plants make the most of the warmth of summer. Many types of plants flower within days of the snow melting in spring and produce seeds in just over a month. Others, such as heathers, do not produce seeds every year, but spread by growing underground stems through the thawing soil.

Growing low

Tundra plants are mostly small to stop them being knocked over by winds. For example, the Arctic willow is related to tall willow trees of warmer biomes but it is usually less than 30 cm tall and grows horizontally, covering many metres of ground.

Lichens are formed from a partnership between spongy fungi and tiny plant-like algae. The fungi support and protect the algae which make food for the fungi. In Arctic tundra, some lichens, such as reindeer lichens, form a crust over many rocks and soil. They can grow all year round in low temperatures and survive being completely frozen and dried out for years.

Caribou can sniff out lichens buried up to 60 cm under snow. They dig it up using their hooves and antlers.

Amazing Adaptation

Caribou are one of the few animals that can survive on lichens. Bacteria in their stomachs help them break down this unusual food and get energy from it.

SURVIVING THE COLD

Tundra animals have some surprising and ingenious ways of surviving in a place where temperatures are as cold as most freezers.

Smaller is better

Many tundra animals have smaller body parts than usual. For example, animals in the Arctic, such as hares, foxes, wolves and bears, have small ears, legs and even tails in comparison to similar animals in warmer places. The reason is that body parts with a smaller surface area lose heat more slowly than parts with a bigger surface area.

Wood frogs can survive being frozen in winter. They stop breathing and their hearts stop beating for weeks at a time until the ice melts and they emerge again in spring!

Stop freezing

Most living things are nearly three quarters water and in freezing tundra conditions this water could turn to ice which can cause damage to body tissues. Some tundra animals, including insects like mosquitoes, and frogs, make their own antifreeze chemicals. These stop the water in their bodies freezing so they can survive the chill.

Amazing Adaptation

Wood frogs lay their eggs in water. If tundra ponds freeze before their eggs hatch, the jelly of the frogspawn freezes fast. This sucks water out of the developing frog inside so it survives the chill.

Warm coats

If you visited a tundra biome in winter you would dress up warm. Many tundra mammals, including wolves, foxes and lemmings, have a permanent warm coat of hair. Musk oxen are giants of the tundra that keep warm even when covered with snow, thanks to their shaggy coat of long hair. Each hair is hollow, and fatter at the tip than at the base. This special shape traps a layer of air warmed by the animal's body. The trapped air insulates the ox's skin from the cold air outside.

The outer hairs are very long and waterproof, too. This forms a kind of warming tent around their body.

The musk ox's large, hard hooves also help it survive. During the winter months, the musk ox uses its hooves to break through ice so it can drink the water underneath.

To make sure they stay warm, musk oxen huddle together in blizzards to share their body heat.

GOING UNDERGROUND

Some tundra animals escape the harsh winters by staying in the same area, but going underground to stay warm.

A sticky situation

Lemmings are animals the size of small guinea pigs that usually keep out of sight of predators by running about the tundra in tunnels and resting in burrows. In summer, the burrows are under deep grass or shrubs, but in winter they are under the snow.

Groups of lemmings choose deep but loose snow to burrow into, rather than snow that is packed tight. The loose snow traps air making it a better insulation layer. Temperatures in burrows under the soft snow blanket are about 7°C warmer than the temperature of the air above the snow.

If a predator comes near a lemming outside the burrow, the plucky little animal shrieks and runs at it with teeth bared to try to scare it off!

Fact Focus: Finding a New Home

In summer, lemmings sometimes leave their underground hiding places in their hundreds and move to new places on the surface. This happens if so many young have been born that there is not enough food to go around in their current home.

Shutting down

Other tundra animals spend winter in a sleep-like state called hibernation. They prepare for this by stuffing themselves with enough food to get fat and by making a burrow where they will remain warm and hidden.

Arctic ground squirrels fatten up on roots, seeds, berries and grasses. They line their burrows with dry grasses, fur, moss and sedges. Then they settle down for winter and go into a deep sleep. During hibernation their hearts slow down from 400 beats per minute to 10, their body cools, and they breathe 20 times more slowly. They use 98 per cent less energy by hibernating than staying awake through winter.

Amazing Adaptation

Brown bears do not hibernate but they do spend the winter months in a den. They go in and out of a deep sleep and survive mostly by using up their body fat. By spring, many have lost a third of their body weight.

Arctic ground squirrels like this one spend up to seven months of the tundra year curled up in hibernation in their burrows.

SEASONAL CHANGES

When spring and summer arrive in the Arctic tundra, there is a transformation from snowy wasteland to busy biome.

Moving in

With warmer weather the snow melts. Plants grow new shoots and masses of insects, such as flies, emerge from winter resting places, breed and lay eggs. Some animals, such as caribou and geese, migrate to the tundra in spring from places with warmer winters to feed on the young plants. They may return to the same feeding grounds each year.

Raising young

Birds, such as terns and plovers, migrate to quiet tundra areas in spring and summer to have their young. They make nests from grasses on the snow-free land. The chicks that hatch feed on insects and new shoots. Within a few months the young birds are ready to fly and migrate to warmer places further south to escape the chills of winter.

Snow geese make nests on the thawed tundra land to rear young. They need to keep careful watch to stop Arctic foxes stealing their precious eggs.

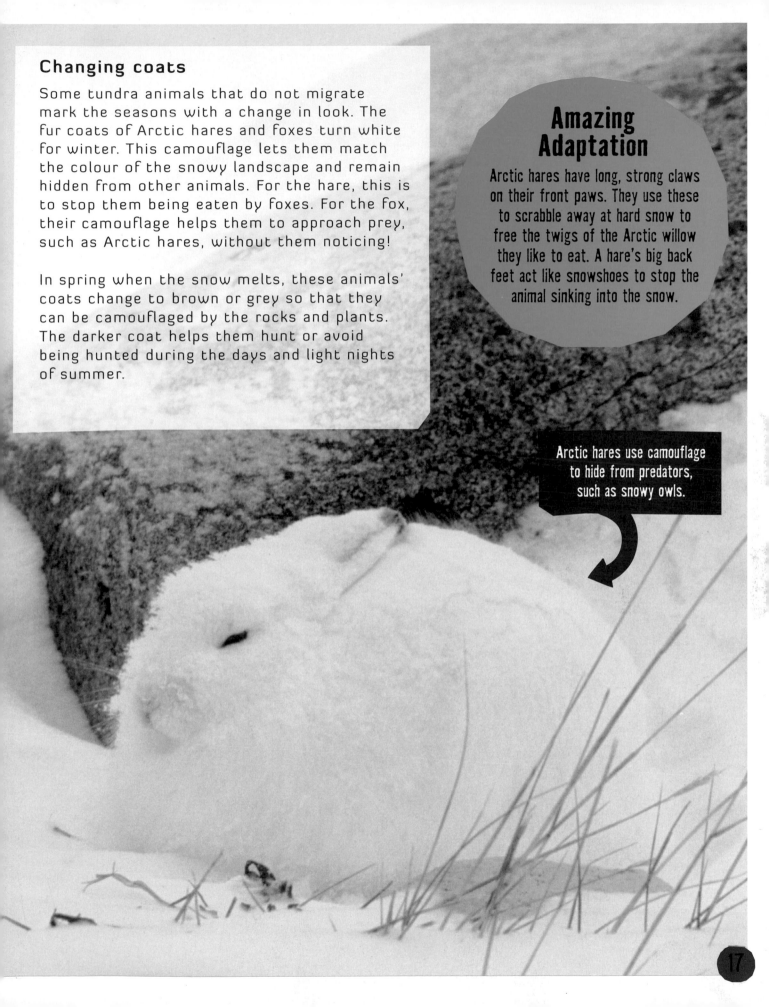

Changing coats

Some tundra animals that do not migrate mark the seasons with a change in look. The fur coats of Arctic hares and foxes turn white for winter. This camouflage lets them match the colour of the snowy landscape and remain hidden from other animals. For the hare, this is to stop them being eaten by foxes. For the fox, their camouflage helps them to approach prey, such as Arctic hares, without them noticing!

In spring when the snow melts, these animals' coats change to brown or grey so that they can be camouflaged by the rocks and plants. The darker coat helps them hunt or avoid being hunted during the days and light nights of summer.

Amazing Adaptation

Arctic hares have long, strong claws on their front paws. They use these to scrabble away at hard snow to free the twigs of the Arctic willow they like to eat. A hare's big back feet act like snowshoes to stop the animal sinking into the snow.

Arctic hares use camouflage to hide from predators, such as snowy owls.

TUNDRA LIFE CYCLES

Getting the timing right in having young can make the difference between survival and death in the tundra.

Protecting babies

Some tundra animals go to great lengths to protect their vulnerable babies from the cold winters. A pregnant polar bear spends summer feeding and fattening up by eating seals on coasts. In autumn, she walks inland and digs out a den big enough for her to turn around in within a snowdrift or bank of soft soil. She waits for snow to shut her inside the den.

The polar bear gives birth usually to two cubs in November or December. She feeds the cubs with her milk for around three months before they are strong enough to leave the den in warmer spring weather. Then the cubs and mother head off for the long walk to find food.

Towards the end of the cubs' time in the den, mum may go on brief, local hunting trips for snacks, such as Arctic hares or lemmings, to share with her babies.

Fact File: Wapusk National Park

Location: Manitoba, Canada
Size: 115,000 km²
Overview: One of the best places on Earth to see polar bears emerging from dens in the spring, but also thousands of caribou and rare birds, such as great grey owls and sandhill cranes.

More or less

Some tundra animals only ever have young if there is enough food to feed them. Snowy owls lay fewer eggs in summers when they cannot find enough lemmings to eat. Lemmings are these birds' favourite prey (even though they also eat other animals, such as ducklings). In an average year a snowy owl may eat 1,600 lemmings!

In years when there are few lemmings, the owls will not make nests or lay any eggs at all. Instead, they fly off to live in the nearest forest where there is a wider range of prey.

Snowy owl chicks are big, fluffy and very hungry. They cannot survive unless the parents can find enough food to feed them.

Fact Focus: Snowy Owl Parents

Snowy owls usually pair up for life. They share duties — hunting day and night to feed their young and will defend their babies against any predators, even wolves.

EAT OR BE EATEN

The animals of any biome rely on each other for survival.
Food chains tell the story of who eats who in a tundra biome.

Start of the chain

Plants start all food chains. Tundra plants trap the energy in sunlight in their leaves using the process of photosynthesis. This makes sugary food for the plant using carbon dioxide from the air and water. Plants use this food to fuel their growth. This slows or stops during long winters when there is much less sunlight.

Amazing Adaptation

Hairs on Alpine butterwort leaves have sticky tips that trap tiny tundra flies. The leaves release chemicals that dissolve the trapped insects and then soak up this fly soup as extra food.

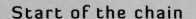

Plant eaters

The tundra animals that eat plants range from tiny insects called springtails to massive musk oxen. Eating and digesting leaves, stems, berries and other parts of plants releases energy and nutrients. So, the energy transfers from plant to plant eater to help the animals stay healthy, grow, develop and produce young.

The Alpine ibex is totally reliant on eating Alpine plants for its survival.

Meat eaters

When different tundra animals eat the plant eaters, energy transfers from plant eaters to meat eaters. Tundra spiders spin webs on plants to catch flies and Arctic wolves work in teams to kill large musk oxen. When prey are not easy to find, tundra hunters may scavenge by eating any dead animals or remains they find. Maggots, worms and slugs tuck into hunters' and scavengers' leftovers.

End of the chain

All food chains end with decomposers. These are bacteria and fungi that break down dead animal remains, dung, dead leaves and other natural waste into nutrients. Nutrients in the tundra soil help plants grow and remain healthy. Energy transfers back to the soil so new food chains can begin.

A wolf defends the dead deer it has found to eat from other tundra scavengers.

Fact Focus: Food Webs

Every biome has hundreds of food chains that are connected in food webs. For example, an Arctic hare eats different plants, and is eaten itself by Arctic wolves and foxes, snowy owls and stoats.

21

PEOPLE IN THE TUNDRA

The tundra may be one of the coldest, toughest biomes on Earth, but there are many groups of people living in tundra habitats.

Tundra living

Groups of indigenous people, such as Nenets and Inuit, have lived in the Arctic tundra for thousands of years. They have traditionally survived by hunting for food, such as seal meat, and wearing sealskin clothing. Some Nenets, people of Siberia, migrate with herds of caribou between winter and summer feeding grounds. These Nenets keep the caribou healthy and safe from wolves. They also kill caribou to eat the meat and drink the blood.

Changing societies

In the Arctic tundra many indigenous people's ways of life have changed. They often use skidoos to get around rather than sledges. Many people live in busy towns and cities, such as Aklavik in Canada, and they may work in shops, restaurants and industries instead of hunting and selling caribou.

Some Nenets people use caribou to pull their sledges. They sew caribou skins together to make warm coats.

New arrivals

Miners, oil workers and builders are some of the people who come to live and work in the Arctic tundra each year, especially during the warmer summer months.

Tourists visit the tundra to see the awe-inspiring scenery and to watch animals in their natural habitats, such as the caribou migrations, rather than in zoos or wildlife parks. They can also enjoy skiing and snow sports in mountain tundra, and learn more about traditional life in Arctic tundra.

People can enjoy watching the colourful display of the Northern Lights from the comfort of a tourist lodge in the Arctic tundra.

Fact Focus: Nature's Light Displays

The Northern Lights are an amazing natural light show people can often see in the Arctic tundra. They are caused by a special wind from the Sun hitting the Earth's atmosphere.

23

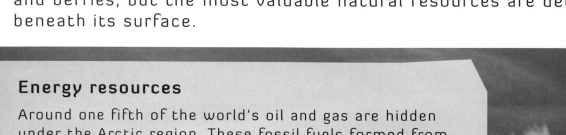

TUNDRA RESOURCES

In the tundra, people can collect wild foods, such as fish and berries, but the most valuable natural resources are deep beneath its surface.

Energy resources

Around one fifth of the world's oil and gas are hidden under the Arctic region. These fossil fuels formed from ancient sea creatures that were squashed and heated inside deep, heavy layers of rock for millions of years.

Oil is made into petroleum which is burnt in engines to make cars and aeroplanes move. Gas is burned in power stations to make electricity and also to heat homes. Companies dig deep wells in the Arctic tundra to get oil and gas from underground. They move the fossil fuels south to places where more people live through very long pipes or on ships.

The Trans–Alaskan oil pipeline snakes for thousands of kilometres across the Arctic tundra biome.

Fact Focus: Caribou Crossing

Oil and gas pipelines are raised on stilts into the air where they cross caribou migration routes. The caribou can then continue on their way without having to climb over giant pipes.

24

Minerals

Fossil fuels are not the only hidden resources in the tundra. People also mine rich deposits of crystals, such as diamonds and amethyst, and metals from rocks at the surface and beneath the permafrost. The metals include iron, which is vital for making steel, and titanium, which is used to make aircraft bodies, white paint and golf clubs!

History in ice

Tundra permafrost is an important resource for scientists. They drill into permafrost to collect samples of ancient soil. Studying the soil can help scientists know what the tundra biome was like in the past. Bubbles of air trapped in ice reveal secrets about the Earth's atmosphere thousands of years ago. Sometimes people even find frozen fossils of ancient animals, such as mammoths, when permafrost melts.

People use giant, heavy machines to mine rock rich in iron minerals in the tundra.

TUNDRA THREATS

The tundra is important and also very useful to people, but we are at risk of damaging it and destroying parts of it forever.

Melting permafrost

Temperatures on Earth are rising because of global warming. This is changing climates worldwide and causing more Arctic ice to melt each year. As permafrost melts, the soil is getting softer, deeper down. This is causing buildings and roads to sink into the ground. The melting is also releasing gases that were trapped in bubbles in frozen soil and gases that bacteria make when eating thawed-out plant waste. These gases are causing more global warming.

Melting permafrost affects animals too. For example, caribou have broad, soft hooves to walk on snow without sinking. But global warming is melting snow in the tundra earlier in the year, so migrating caribou end up walking on hard, painful rock instead.

These buildings in Yukon, Canada have slumped together because their foundations have sunk into the softened permafrost.

Pollution problems

Pollution is also a problem in the tundra. When oil spills from pipelines or chemicals used to process metals wash from mines, living things are harmed or even die. People spray chemicals called pesticides to kill irritating mosquitoes near tundra towns in summer. Unfortunately, the pesticides also poison tundra birds when they eat lots of mosquitoes.

Damage done

When the tundra landscape is damaged, it is slow to recover. Major damage is caused by building new roads, railways, mines and towns. But even minor damage, such as bike or skidoo tracks, ski runs and footprints can take centuries to recover. This is because the top layer of soil washes away as the permafrost melts below.

Some people hunt and kill beautiful tundra wildlife. Too much hunting is making some types of animal, such as the Arctic wolf, rare.

People damage the Arctic tundra when they construct new buildings on it.

Fact Focus: Predators and People

When Arctic tundra is disturbed or damaged there are fewer prey to hunt. Dangerous predators, such as polar bears, brown bears and wolves, may go into towns to find food.

TUNDRA FUTURES

Tundra is a remarkable and fascinating biome. That's why people are taking action to protect tundra now and into the future.

Reserves

One way people protect tundra biomes is by creating reserves. In reserves, there are controls to limit building and mining. This ensures animals can migrate without having to cross roads and can raise young safely without being disturbed. Pollution can be prevented by banning industries, such as oil drilling.

When tourists visit reserves their money is used to help the reserve and to pay the wages of local people. Visitors also learn about the biome and how to protect it, for example, by only using marked paths and roads tourists reduce the damage to delicate tundra plants and soil.

Walkers rest near the mosses of mountain tundra in Svalbard, Norway. All plants are protected in this fragile place so tourists must take special care not to damage them.

Fact Focus: The Loss of Lichen

Lichens can be damaged and die if there is too much air pollution. When industries reduce air pollution, there are more tundra lichens for plant eaters, from tiny insects to caribou.

Changing energy use

Global warming is affecting all biomes and settlements on our planet in different ways. The biggest change that people can make to slow the warming is by reducing their use of fossil fuels. They can reduce power use, such as turning off lights when leaving rooms or using energy-efficient washing machines.

People can use vehicles less by walking and cycling more, sharing car trips and taking fewer flights. What can you do to help?

The Arctic National Wildlife Refuge is the biggest wildlife reserve in the USA and home to a huge variety of animals including beautiful grizzly bears like these.

Fact File: Arctic National Wildlife Refuge

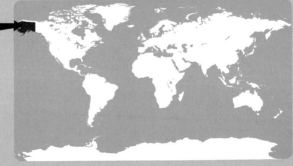

Location: Alaska, USA
Size: 80,000 km²
Overview: A protected home to 250 species of animal, such as caribou, wolves and polar bears. Oil companies want to drill in the coastal region because there is lots of oil beneath the ground.

GLOSSARY

adaptation special feature or behaviour that helps a living thing survive in its habitat.

algae living thing similar to a plant that makes its own food by photosynthesis.

antifreeze chemical added to water to stop it freezing.

Arctic region including the North Pole, Arctic Ocean and the land surrounding it

bacteria tiny living things that can cause diseases or decompose waste.

biome region of Earth with living things adapted to the typical climate, soils and other features.

breeding having young.

bud plant part that contains young flowers, leaves or shoots.

camouflage colour, pattern or shape that makes it hard to identify an object against its background.

caribou large, hairy animal with hooves and antlers, also known as reindeer.

climate typical weather pattern through the year in an area

decomposer living things, such as bacteria and fungi, that break down waste and bits of dead plants and animals into nutrients.

dissolve mix a solid with a liquid so much that it has become part of the liquid.

food chain way of showing what animal eats what in a place.

food web feeding relationships between living things, usually in a particular habitat or biome

fossil fuel oil, gas and coal, fuels which formed millions of years ago inside rocks from the remains of living things.

fungi type of living thing, such as mushrooms or yeasts

global warming rise in average temperature of Earth caused by human activity, which is altering weather patterns.

habitat place where an animal or plant typically lives.

hibernation special type of deep sleep when body processes slow down.

indigenous people who have lived in a place for a very long time and have strong historical, cultural and other associations with it.

insulation layer that prevents the loss of heat from an object or living thing.

lichen life-form that is a partnership between two types of living things, fungi and algae.

meltwater water created when ice melts.

migrate move from one area to another due to seasonal changes.

national park an area in nature where the wildlife is protected by law.

natural resources things found in nature that are useful to people, such as plants and water.

nutrient chemical substances essential for living things to be healthy, grow and live.

permafrost deep layer of permanently frozen soil

pesticide chemical used to kill pest insects and other animals.

photosynthesis process by which green plants make sugary food using the energy in sunlight.

pollinate transfer grains called pollen from one flower to another so a plant can make seeds.

pollution something that damages water, air or land or makes it harmful to living things

predator animal that hunts and eat others.

prey animals hunted and eaten by others.

reserve area protected to keep living things and landscapes of interest safe from people.

scavenger animal who feeds on dead things or waste.

sedges grass-like plants with tough stems

skidoo a snowmobile or motorised sledge.

stilt pole used to raise something above ground.

surface area area on the outside of an object

thaw become liquid or soft after warming up.

treeline line beyond which it is too dry or cold for trees to grow.

FIND OUT MORE

Books

Travelling Wild: Expedition to the Arctic
Alex Woolfe, Wayland, 2014

A Caribou Journey
Debbie S. Miller and Jon Van Zyle,
University of Chicago Press, 2014

Arctic Tundra (Earth's Last Frontiers)
Ellen Labrecque, Raintree, 2015

Baby Mammoth Mummy: Frozen in Time: A Prehistoric Animal's Journey into the 21st Century (National Geographic Kids)
Christopher Sloan, National Geographic Society 2011

WEBSITES AND WEBCAMS

For more facts and information about tundra, go to:
www.blueplanetbiomes.org/tundra.htm,
kids.nceas.ucsb.edu/biomes/tundra.html and
www.ucmp.berkeley.edu/glossary/gloss5/biome/tundra.html

Arctic foxes are fascinating tundra animals. Learn more at:
www.arkive.org/arctic-fox/vulpes-lagopus/image-G58212.html

The caribou migration is remarkable. Find out more about it at:
www.fws.gov/refuge/arctic/carcon.html

Discover more about the traditional lives of Nenets people at:
www.survivalinternational.org/photo-stories/3198-the-nenets-of-siberia

Webcams

Watch polar bears going about their daily lives in the Arctic tundra from the warmth of your home! The video is filmed from a buggy that carries scientists and tourists.
explore.org/live-cams/player/polar-bear-tundra-buggy-cam

instaar.colorado.edu/tundracam/ is a steerable web cam! You can use it to look around an area of mountain tundra in Colorado, USA. Maybe you'll see a moose walking past...

INDEX